THE RISE OF CRYPTOCURRENCIES

The Beginner's Guide of Investing and Understanding Cryptocurrencies

BY: TONY GIGGS

Congratulations!!!

You have just downloaded "The Rise of Cryptocurrencies: The Beginner's Guide of Investing and Understanding Cryptocurrencies" . With the help of this book you will be totally on point with cryptocurrencies . This book will guide you every step of the way , you won't need any other book after this one . This book has it all . From what to invest in to how cryptocurrencies work .

I really hope you enjoy this book and please if you would be kind enough to leave a review . I would highly appreciate that . Thank You !

You are now a step closer to become a successful *Cryptocurrency Investor* !

Please checkout all my other books on Amazon . Thank you ! **ENJOY** !!!

Table of Contents

Introduction 1

Chapter 1: The history of cryptocurrency 3

Chapter 2: Why should you use cryptocurrency 5

Chapter 3: Blockchain Technology 8

Chapter 4: Currency vs. Money 11

Chapter 5: The Top Cryptocurrencies 15

Chapter 6: Why Bitcoin is a good currency 22

Chapter 7: Cryptocurrency Wallets 25

Chapter 8: The Basics of Mining 28

Chapter 9: Bitcoin Investing Strategies 32

Chapter 10: Trading and Investing 34

Chapter 11: How to Invest in Cryptocurrency 42

Chapter 12: Benefits and Risks of Investing 46

Chapter 13: Cryptocurrency Broker 52

Chapter 14: Strategies for Risk Minimization 57

Chapter 15: Powerful Strategies 61

Conclusion 67

INTRODUCTION

A cryptocurrency is a form of digital cash that has high security. It is stored electronically (online); therefore, it does not have a physical existence. In most cases, a high level of anonymity is also enjoyed by its users. It functions as a substitute for money but also offers other interesting features. It is secured using cryptography, which refers to the process of converting information into codes. Cryptography was used during the Second World War when it was important for an army to ensure the privacy and security of communication against enemies. As the world evolved into the digital and computer era, cryptography found its application in the world of cryptocurrency.

It is possible to create cryptocurrencies that are independent of governments and central banks. Such currencies are decentralized in the way the inventors intended them to be. When we look at the history of cryptocurrencies, we shall see that such independence was a major driver in the creation of cryptocurrencies.

Some central banks have found great uses for the underlying technology, but any resulting currency not is cryptocurrency, as envisaged by its original creators. Any such currency coming from governments or banks will be centralized, and the original creators of cryptocurrency were completely opposed to such centralization.

Although a cryptocurrency normally functions as a substitute for money, it is noteworthy that people who have cryptocurrencies do not always use them as such. These days, many people own cryptocurrencies as a form of investment. This is because putting your money in cryptocurrencies can be a very lucrative investment. Unlike investing in stocks where an annual profit of 30% is already considered high, you can profit by more than 200% (or even more) in a month's time when you invest in cryptocurrency. In fact, there are already many people around the world who have earned millions just by investing in cryptocurrencies. Even if you compare it with other investments, it is easy to realize that investing in cryptocurrency is most likely the best option that can help you achieve financial freedom. This is also the reason why many investors in stocks, bonds, and real estate, have turned to investing in cryptocurrencies.

CHAPTER 1

THE HISTORY OF CRYPTOCURRENCY

During the year 1998, b-money was published by Wei Dai as an anonymously distributed digital currency. It was not too long after that, Nick Szabo, came up with the cryptocurrency Bitgold.

Similar to Bitcoin and various other cryptocurrencies, Bitgold was a system that would require the users to provide proof of work for the algorithm that they solved along with their solutions so that they could be published together before they were rewarded for the work that they did. A reusable proof of work system was created by Mr. Hal Finney as he followed in the footsteps of Dai and Szabo.

Bitcoin was created in 2009 by Satoshi Nakamoto – this is a pseudonym for the developer –. This digital currency was designed to use a hash function known as SHA-256 as well as the proof of work scheme that was created by Finney.

A few years later, Namecoin was released in an attempt to create a decentralized DNS; the purpose behind the decentralization was to make internet censorship more difficult.

Peercoin was one of the first cryptocurrencies to be able to use proof of stake and proof of work thus making it a hybrid currency. IOTA was another currency, but it was not based on the blockchain. Instead, it used Tangle.

During the year of 2014, the United Kingdom announced the Department of the Treasury was going to be conducting a study on cryptocurrencies and how they would affect the economy. This study was conducted to determine if there needed to be regulations on cryptocurrency or not.

CHAPTER 2

WHY SHOULD YOU USE CRYPTOCURRENCY

Using cryptocurrency is a good step in creating global trade. But, there are some other reasons as to why you should be using cryptocurrency.

1. It is going to be risk-free for sellers. Whenever payments are taken by allowing the customer to pay with cryptocurrency, the transaction cannot be reversed. This means that a merchant is no longer going to need to worry about a payment being stopped and them not receiving their money. Therefore, blockchain makes it to where it is almost impossible for a seller to be defrauded.

2. Since miners are going to be rewarded for their work in cryptocurrency by the network, then there is not going to be a transaction fee; and if there is a fee, but, the fee is not going

to be as much as it typically would if you were using the traditional banking system.

3. Almost everyone has access to the internet in some form or fashion. However, not everyone is going to be able to access a bank or a money exchange system. By using cryptocurrency, you are going to be receiving payments electronically and will not need to deal with a bank or worry about a line of credit.

4. As long as you have the digital key that you are provided when you set up your cryptocurrency wallet, you are going to be able to access the currency that is yours and yours alone. This is going to be different than using a bank because you are not going to be limited in accessing of your assets and they are not going to be able to be frozen by any entity.

5. You already know that when you pay with a credit card or a debit card, you are going to be giving the merchant access to sensitive banking information. However, cryptocurrency is going to be sent directly to the recipient without any information being submitted except for the public key and the amount that you are sending.

The risks of cryptocurrency

Any investment is going to have a risk tied to it. Cryptocoins are going to hold a host of vulnerabilities that you are going to need to be aware of before you can start investing in cryptocurrency.

1. While a hacker is not going to be able to hack the blockchain, they are going to be able to hack your wallet and even the cryptocurrency exchanges. The most recent hack occurred in 2016 where over $50 million in ether was taken from investors in the DAO fund.

2. The prices of cryptocurrency will be volatile just like any other stock that you would be trading. With the DAO being hacked, the price of ether fell drastically, and this lead to a market correction that had to happen.

3. Do not invest all your savings in cryptocurrency. That is one of the things that people often think that they have to do whenever it comes to investing in any sort of stock. You need to ensure that you are going to be able to survive should you lose everything that you have invested. When it comes to cryptocurrency, you are going to have to worry about someone getting into your wallet and stealing all your coins.

CHAPTER 3

BLOCKCHAIN TECHNOLOGY

Blockchain Technology represents the first successful implementation of the DLT framework, and while there are more of such implementations being developed, there is no denying that they will have to be extra special to knock the blockchain off its perch.

A Blockchain is essentially a network of computing nodes having the same copies of a mutually shared database (distributed ledger) in which updates and changes to the records stored in the database are made using a majority consensus based upon some predefined mathematical rules. Each transaction forms a "block" which is linked to other transaction blocks forming the blockchain. In its most basic form, a blockchain can be imagined to be an infinitely long chain made up of transaction blocks all the way down to the first transaction block in the chain known as the Genesis Block. As usual, let us break down this seemingly complex definition.

It begins with understanding what a network is. When two or more computers share information with one another, a network is formed. In the blockchain network, the information being shared is the single mutually distributed ledger which is replicated and shared to all the participating network nodes (computers). When a new computer connects to the blockchain, it sends a request to the nearest available node (peer) to gain access to the distributed ledger. Depending on the protocols set up within the blockchain network, there are many types of nodes present in a blockchain network. Some nodes maintain a full copy of the distributed ledger, there are others that hold an abridged copy, and there are some solely responsible for validating transactions.

The relationship between blockchain network and cryptocurrencies has been likened to what the internet is to email. Simply put, blockchain network is the technology that cryptocurrency transactions are built on, and that simplifies our transactions. It is a numerical or digital (online) ledger that records transactions that are made in cryptocurrencies, sequentially and openly. It is different from the current way of banking, where all transactions are linked to a non-visible, centralized network. But the blockchain technology is a decentralized database of the digital ledger, and it is made public for all to see. So, it makes it possible to monitor every transaction into details. It is distributed in that, even in the comfort of your room, you can control all your transaction transparently. Each transaction is viewed as a single block, where subsequent transactions or blocks are added to make a digital, linear, chronological chain known as blockchain. Each time a block is completed, a new block is automatically generated. Each computer connected to this network is called a node. So, when a new transaction is recorded, a copy of the blockchain is sent to each node as they join the network. This decentralized database of the digital ledger is replicated and harmonized through the internet by anyone connected, so it renders useless the use of a centralized administrator (like banks). This digital ledger is incorruptible (no centralized information available for alteration or hacking) and it records not only financial dealing but also anything that has value (assets).

CHAPTER 4

CURRENCY VS. MONEY

Digital Currency

Money dealt with using electronic systems is digital currency. This kind of money is called virtual money or cybercash. Every unit of virtual money can be mapped to a memory block in some digital storage device like a hard disk. It is essentially stored and transferred over the internet using network servers and databases. There are many advantages to this type of transactions. For instance, unlike physical transfer of cash which can be a hassle sometimes(risky, time-consuming, transaction fee, etc.), digital transactions over the internet can be not only safe but also instantaneous provided the right software is used.

There are multiple forms of digital currency.

Virtual Currency is a digital representation of money which is purely online, i.e., it does not have a physical counterpart. It essentially consists of virtual assets(called digital money) that are not regulated by a central financial authority. So the reach and usage are limited to specific online communities that accept it.

Cryptocurrency is a digital currency in which the money is stored, transferred and verified using cryptographic techniques. It is also a virtual currency. So the individual monetary units of the cryptocurrency(e.g., bitcoins) are created and safeguarded using complex encryption/decryption algorithms. Many cryptocurrency systems are decentralized, i.e., they are not controlled by a central bank or government authority. We will look into the effectiveness of cryptocurrencies in further chapters.

Currency and money aren't synonyms though they are used synonymously. If you look the meanings of these words up in a thesaurus, they will indeed be listed as a synonym. However, their economic functioning is different. In this chapter, you will understand the difference between these two so that you can preserve your wealth.

Money

Money is referred to as commodity money, and the commodity could be anything ranging from seashells to stones. This is a medium of exchange that is used for buying and selling goods and services, and for the repayment of debt as well. Precious metals are finite, but flat currency is capable of being printed according to the government's desires. Gold is absolute, whereas flat currencies aren't. These precious metals cannot be created nor destroyed, only transformed and they can exist forever. You cannot apply the same concept to the paper money you carry with you. Fiat currencies are inherently transient, and their value depends on the rise and fall of their nations.

Gold standard

While paper money started getting popular in Europe, people were still using coins for buying and selling stuff up till the 17th century. To discourage people from using gold directly and use paper notes instead, a monetary system called the gold standard was put in place. Paper notes issued by the government were equated with the appropriate fixed amount of gold. For example, 100 notes would have the same value as 1 gram of gold. And this was bound in law and protected by the government so that people could trade and exchange value with notes instead of gold.

The British West Indies(now divided into separate countries) was one of the first provinces to adopt a gold standard. In 1717, Sir Isaac Newton who was the master of the Royal Mint set a new silver-to-gold mint ratio, and this drove out silver from the circulated currency and established a gold standard for Britain.

Although many countries still hold gold reserves, the system of the gold standard has been abandoned. The U.S government led by President Nixon gave up the gold standard in 1971 which means that you can no longer uphold the government(and private banks) to exchange dollars for the equivalent amount of gold. Since 1971, the U.S has been using a fiat currency system for representing its money.

Currency

For most, currency or fiat currency refers to the hard earned cash or cash in hand. It includes dollars, pounds, euros, yen, and all other types of the physical currency note that you can keep in your wallet. The primary medium of economic exchange in a country is currency, and it could be in the form of paper or coins. The currency was made of precious metals, and these materials were quite difficult to transport. The idea was to create a kind of movable currency that would serve the same purpose and was backed up by precious metals. For instance, banknotes are usually backed by precious metals like gold or silver. These banknotes can be exchanged for their legal tender anytime. Legal tender refers to the precious metals that back such notes. The US silver certificates can be exchanged for their worth in silver. The US adopted the gold standard in 1879, and since then the currency is backed by certain precious metals that lend credibility to the issuing government. People accepted this currency system since they knew their wealth was secured by the precious metals backing it.

CHAPTER 5

THE TOP CRYPTOCURRENCIES

It is common for people to refer to two basic cryptocurrency variants; Bitcoins and Altcoins. Altcoins are all other non-Bitcoin cryptocurrencies. In this context, Bitcoin is given legacy status being the first fully implemented cryptocurrency. Please note that all market capitalization and trading values given for the cryptocurrencies are accurate as of mid-September 2017.

1. Bitcoin (BTC)

The Bitcoin, created by the anonymous scientist, Satoshi Nakamoto in 2008, is one of the pioneers of digital currency and can be used to purchase items over the internet (electronically) and Eve in some cases locally. Now it is interesting to find out that you don't need to understand everything about the technicalities of the Bitcoin before you can start using it as a means of exchange. Just install the bitcoin wallet on your electronic device, maybe a computer or a smartphone. It will automatically generate a bitcoin address for you once this is done, and then you can proceed to perform real transactions, in fact, all types of transactions with it. As your need for more transactions increases, you can generate more Bitcoin addresses for yourself. For an in-depth look at Bitcoin, you can check out "Bitcoin: The Complete Guide To Understanding Bitcoin" you can get it here: http://cryptocurrencystudio.com/bitcoin

2. Ether (ETH)

One of the newest parts of the blockchain is Ethereum, which has gained large popularity in 2017, becoming the second most traded cryptocurrency. Ethereum is a software platform that's decentralized which was released in 2015. It is something that enables distributed applications and smart contacts to be built without control, downtime, or any form of fraud. So more than just being a part of the blockchain, Ethereum also acts as a programming language that completely runs on the blockchain, and is responsible for helping developers improve and publish more blockchain mechanisms— so that the future of blockchain will certainly be brighter.

3. Ripples (XRP)

"Ripples" is the name given to the cryptocurrency for the Ripple Transaction Protocol (RXTP) which is an RTGS (Real-Time Gross Settlement System). It was released in 2012 as part of a collaborative effort between a few developers and Ryan Fugger who created Ripplepay in 2004. It has found a lot of success within mainstream financial institutions where some have adopted it in their payment infrastructure technology. It has a market capitalization of $9 billion with a trading value of $0.19

4. Bitcoin Cash (BCH2)

Bitcoin Cash was launched in August of 2017 and a little over a month, its value has risen astronomically that many investors are beginning to see it as a real contender to Bitcoin for the tag of "most valuable cryptocurrency." Its current market capital capitalization stands at $8 billion which is beyond impressive for a one-month-old cryptocurrency. It also currently trades at about $475. Bitcoin Cash was created as a result of a "hard fork" in the original Bitcoin blockchain due to disagreements centered on the implementation of Bitcoin Improvement Proposal (BIP) 91. This BIP was for the introduction of Segregated Witness (SegWit) which brought up issues relating to maximum block-size limits. As a result, the Bitcoin Cash was implemented by those who were dissatisfied with proceedings, and the hard fork was initiated on August 1, 2017. Bitcoin Cash inherited the Bitcoin Blockchain up until the hard fork which happened at block 478558. So, from block 478559, the Bitcoin Cash Blockchain became different from the original Bitcoin Blockchain.

5. Litecoin (LTC)

Charles Lee, a former Google engineer, unveiled Litecoin. Litecoin was introduced as the "silver" to the "gold" of Bitcoin. Lee had come up with the idea of Litecoin to fix the problems that Bitcoins posed.

Litecoin doesn't get issued by a government like other currencies. The government has singularly been the entity throughout the history that has been responsible for minting money. The Federal Reserve doesn't regulate Litecoins, and they aren't minted by a press at the Bureau of Engraving and Printing. A complicated process referred to as mining instead creates Litecoins. This process comprises the processing and verification of several Litecoin transactions. Unlike fiat currency, there is a cap on the number of Litecoins present. There can be no more than 84 million Litecoins in circulation. A block is generated on the Litecoin network in every 2.5 minutes. The block is made up of ledger entries of Litecoin transactions that take place around the world. This is where a Litecoin derives its value. The block of transactions is verified by using mining software and is visible to any miner who wishes to see it. Once a block is verified, the next block will enter the chain, and this would contain the record of all the Litecoin transactions ever transacted.

6. Dash (DASH)

Originally known as DarkCoin, Dash is also a decentralized peer-to-peer cryptocurrency like Bitcoin albeit a more secretive one. It was launched in January 2014 and experienced a surge in traffic and fan-following quickly. It's famous features include instant transactions (InstantSend) and complete private transactions (PrivateSend). It also uses a separate chained hashing algorithm called X11 unlike bitcoin's SHA256. Market cap for Dash is around 1 billion dollars and one Dash coin will cost you $165 (at of time of this writing).

7. NEM (XEM)

NEM stands for New Economy Movement, and it is the first ever Smart Asset Blockchain implementation. It was released in March of 2015 after the alpha and beta versions had been tested the previous year. It uses a Proof-of-Importance algorithm to validate transactions rather than the popular Proof-of-work/stake used in most other cryptocurrencies. NEM has a market capitalization of $2.1 billion dollars, and it is currently trading at $0.24.

8. IOTA (IOT)

Though still in the open beta testing phase, IOTA has seen some remarkable growth. Created by a group of experts in the blockchain and distributed computing industry, IOTA is one of those cryptocurrencies that have introduced something new and exciting to the cryptocurrency space. IOTA uses a "blockless" distributed ledger (i.e., no transaction blocks linked together in a blockchain). The entire architecture framework looks a lot like a tangled and chaotic mess which is why the technology is called "Tangle," but it is anything but chaotic. Using Directed Acyclic Graph (DAG) as against a traditional blockchain and abandoning the Elliptic Curve Cryptography (ECC) in favor of a much faster hash-based cryptography, transactions in IOTA happen at lightning fast pace making many experts posit that IOTA will be the backbone of the emerging IoT (Internet of Things) technology. IOTA has a market capitalization of $1.6 billion with a trading value of $0.60.

9. Dogecoin

This digital currency was launched in 2013, and it uses a technology of scripts as a proof-of-work scheme. The makeup was based on the same protocol used in creating the Bitcoin, although there were some modifications. There is no limit to the production of this digital currency, and it is best suited for carrying out smaller transactions because this cryptocurrency deals with coins that are lesser values individually. The block time is approximately 60 seconds.

10. NEO(NEO): Neo is a crypto currency, originally called AntShares is, created in China. It has been created to be in sync with Chinese government rulings on cryptocurrency. Like Ethereum, NEO is a platform, which enables the development of smart contracts. NEO has collaborated with Microsoft to create some of its features. The problem of scalability has been taken very seriously and NEO claims to be able to handle 1000 transactions per second and eventually 10,000! This compares very favorably with Bitcoin's 7 transactions per second, and Ethereum's 15 transactions per second. A particularly useful feature of NEO is NeoFS, which involves the storage of large files on nodes in the NEO network. Security has been taken very seriously and it is believed that even quantum computers, when they become common, will be unable to crack the security of the Neo network. NEO is a cryptocurrency

with a market capitalization of more $1.75 billion (US), the value of one NEO is more than $20.

CHAPTER 6

WHY BITCOIN IS A GOOD CURRENCY

1. Divisibility: To measure and grade value, a good currency needs to be divisible to the smallest required scale (e.g., dollars & cents, pounds & sterlings, rupees & paisa). The bitcoin protocol has been designed in such a way that you can divide one bitcoin into many smaller units called Satoshis which can be further divided if necessary.

2. Durability: The whole purpose of currency is to represent money in a physical/virtual form so that people can have an easier time exchanging value. If the currency fades away with time or gets worn out over repeated use, it can be a hassle to keep churning out more currency to replace the damage. All physical currencies are prone to physical damage like wear & tear, weather, etc. This is where bitcoin trumps all other forms of currencies because it is 100% digital. The life-time of a bitcoin is theoretically infinite. It will survive as long as there's an operating network that runs

the bitcoin protocol. A decentralized network, high level of encryption, digitized currency and the existential guarantee of the internet in the foreseeable future make bitcoin one of the most durable currencies ever created.

3. Transferability: If you have a working internet connection and a computer(smartphone or tablet will also work), you can transfer bitcoins with just a couple of clicks. This makes it a very convenient mode of money transfer unlike bank cheques and wire transfers. There is no central authority or third party that charges a transfer fee, so it is also a more profitable mode of money transfer.

4. Interchangeable: We already know that currency is just a set of monetary units in use. As such, a good currency is one in which the units are interchangeable. This means that all the units should be identical in structure and represent the same amount of value. Take gold for example. 1 gram of gold has the same value anywhere. Similarly, 1 bitcoin is the same as the other. For all practical purposes, you can exchange 1 bitcoin with another, and there would be no difference in value.

5. Scarcity: Only 21 million bitcoins can ever exist. We will see why in further chapters. This cap on the total amount of bitcoins ensures that its net value never drops too low. As the economy grows, the value of bitcoin also increases. It is estimated that one bitcoin will be worth around 1 million

dollars in less than 20 years. And it costs less than 3000 dollars at the time of this writing.

CHAPTER 7

CRYPTOCURRENCY WALLETS

Web Wallet

A web wallet is the most common type of cryptocurrency hot wallet. It is the most widely used wallet. It is also referred to as an online wallet. As the name already implies, a web wallet is the kind of cryptocurrency wallet that is accessible on the World Wide Web. A good example of a web wallet is Coinbase.

Desktop Wallet

A desktop wallet is a kind of cold wallet. Hence, it is stored offline. When you use a desktop wallet, you store your cryptocurrency in a computer. Although called as a desktop wallet, the computer that you use does not necessarily have to be a desktop computer. It can also be a laptop, as long as it has a functioning Operating System.

When you use a desktop wallet, you should remember that the computer that you use should not be connected to the Internet. The reason is that once something is connected to the Internet, there is an exposure to risks and possibility of getting hacked. Also, before you use a computer as a desktop wallet, it is strongly suggested that you reformat it to remove bugs and viruses.

Mobile Wallet

A mobile wallet is another type of hot wallet. It is the type of hot wallet that you can download on your mobile device. Many web wallets also have a mobile version. Therefore, it is not unusual to find a web wallet that is also a mobile wallet at the same time. Again, a good example of this would be Coinbase. It is a hot wallet that has an online presence, as well as a mobile feature.

Hardware Wallet

A hardware wallet is also like a desktop wallet. It is also a cold wallet, but instead of storing your cryptocurrencies in a computer, you get to store them in some hardware device, such as a USB. Just like a desktop computer, you should avoid connecting your hardware wallet to a computer that is connected to the Internet.

Paper Wallet

A paper wallet is a kind of cold wallet where you store your private and public keys on a paper. It is a good practice to print several copies of your keys and be sure to keep them in a safe place. Most paper wallets will give you a QR code that you can scan before you can access your wallet online. This way you can rest for sure that your cryptocurrencies are protected since a person will have to get a copy of the codes that you have printed on a paper before he can access your cryptocurrencies which are stored online.

Cold Wallet vs. Hot Wallet

Before you can even start investing in or trading cryptocurrencies, the first step is for you to have a cryptocurrency wallet. A cryptocurrency wallet is where you store your cryptocurrencies. Now, there are different kinds of cryptocurrency wallets. You should know their differences so that you will know which wallet type is most suitable for your needs. There are only two kinds of cryptocurrency wallets. There is a hot wallet and a cold wallet. On the one hand, a hot wallet is the kind of cryptocurrency wallet that exists online. Hence, it is very convenient to use. On the other hand, a cold wallet is the kind of cryptocurrency wallet that is stored offline. Although it is not as convenient to use as a hot wallet, a cold wallet offers greater security since it is not exposed to the Internet. Now, let us take a look at the specific types of cryptocurrency wallets.

CHAPTER 8

THE BASICS OF MINING

How Mining Works

To keep the network running and keep people interested in coins, we have to talk about cryptocurrency mining, which has different forms in how the mining is done and the way the mining works.

We'll talk about how the mining is done here, but we may talk about how the mining works for other cryptocurrencies beyond bitcoin in another book because it usually doesn't matter to the average Bitcoin miner. When you mine a cryptocurrency, what you are doing is you are solving a mathematical problem that the Network gives you to prove a transaction happened. Due to how the blockchain works, each person in the network is given random access to a transaction code that will prove whether a person legitimately got a Bitcoin or not.

Mining is also used to introduce new digital currency into the system. When new coins are created, miners are rewarded with the transaction fees. These new coins are distributed in a decentralized manner, and it builds confidence in the security of the entire system. Miners also assist in keeping the network secure by consensus approval of transactions. Mining ensures fairness while keeping the network safe, secure and stable.

GPU

Now the reason why they switched to the GPU, otherwise known as the graphical processing unit, even though it is specifically built to handle geometry and other shape-based tasks and coloring is that of core count. You see, while the CPU could only ever get an average of 4 to 8 cores, the GPU had an average of 20 to 30 cores at the lower end of the spectrum. GPU core count has gone up significantly in the past decade. Starting at the 10-year mark, we had a graphics card that was the GeForce 7800 GTX with a whopping 24 cores.

Speed up to today, and you have the GeForce GTX 1080 Ti with 3,584 cores. As you can see, you have a massive difference regarding core count, and so once someone developed a method for using GPUs, almost the entire market switched to using it. This had caused some massive problems within the PC community as a brand-new graphics card could cost a respectable $300-$600 before this occurred and now we see prices between $600-$1,000 depending on the power.

CPU

The first and primary hardware that most people began cryptocurrency mining with is the CPU otherwise known as the central processing unit.

The average computer has around 4 cores so that means that the average computer could only solve 4 problems at once. This was significantly slower than the new methods for solving the algorithmic problems but, at this stage in the game, nearly everyone could join the network and make some money. That is until they started using GPU power and while there are still areas that use CPU power, the average basic mining is now done on GPU power.

The CPU is the thinking box of your computer, and it handles all of the very complex calculations that your computer needs to do to make everything work. However, the power of a CPU is significantly limited because it can only run one process for every core that it has. Needless to say, unless you run a server, your average PC will only have a maximum of 16 cores thanks to current technologies.

The New form of Mining: ASICs

Now, the new form of mining revolves around a relatively obscure technology to the rest of society called an ASIC. When it comes to CPU and GPU, nearly any avid PC Gamer on the planet that plays their games on a routine basis will be able to tell you what you need to look for. ASICs are like RVs are to the average person; we might know they exist, we might have been in one, but we probably don't even know the first thing about operating them. ASIC stands for Application Specific Integrated Chip.

CHAPTER 9

BITCOIN INVESTING STRATEGIES

There are three simple steps that you should always follow while investing in Bitcoins.

Price drops are common

Bitcoin is a volatile cryptocurrency, and it can experience several price changes. This is quite common with any investment. The price of a Bitcoin can drop faster than anything else due to its volatile nature. You need to be prepared for any fluctuations in its price. Its value will not be constant and don't get scared when it feels like the price has decreased slightly. This happens because no one knows if this new technology will overthrow the existing financial system or just give it a new makeover.

Always have a plan

If you are interested in becoming a successful investor, then make sure that you always have a strategy in mind. A strategy or a plan would depend on your financial goal. Maybe you want to take up investing in paying off your student debt, for creating a retirement plan, or maybe for some other reason. Having a goal in mind will help you in coming up with a plan with sufficient risk-reward tradeoff. For instance, a student looking to pay off the student loans can invest $100 for now with the potential of repaying the loans off within 4 years. If you are interested in securing your future post-retirement and have a steady job, for now, the amount that you are willing to invest will increase as well. Also, the risk you are willing to take on will differ depending on your goals.

Always secure your Bitcoins

The owner of a Bitcoin has complete control over their funds. Where there is power, responsibility is bound to follow suit. You need to understand that you are probably your worst enemy. It isn't just the threat of hacking and theft that you should be wary of. Selling your Bitcoins at a low price is certainly a bad idea, and panic selling is even worse. Poor investment decisions and lapse of security can incur you a major loss. Your Bitcoins should always be stored in a secure wallet and take utmost care while doing so. Follow all the safety and security protocols. Don't give your private key to anyone. Also, don't forget your security. If you do, then you cannot retrieve your Bitcoins.

CHAPTER 10

TRADING AND INVESTING

Cryptocurrency Exchanges

What does a cryptocurrency exchange mean?

There are certain cryptocurrency websites where you can sell, purchase or trade cryptocurrencies for any other form of digital or traditional currency. These sites are referred to as cryptocurrency exchanges.

Types of exchanges

There are a couple of types of exchanges that you can make use of like-

Direct trading

These websites are designed to offer a direct person-to-person trading platform where individuals from anywhere in the world can gather to exchange currencies. Direct trading exchanges don't have a market price, and instead, each seller has the option of setting their exchange rate.

Trading platforms

All the websites that connect different buyers and sellers. These websites charge a fee for every transaction that takes place.

Brokers

These are the websites that anyone interested in buying cryptocurrencies can visit, and buy the currency at a listed price. Cryptocurrency brokers are quite similar to the dealers of foreign exchange.

Reputation:

The best way to gather information about a particular exchange is to search for it from the reviews given by individual users and also well-known websites providing information about the industry. You can inquire about it on other platforms and forums like Reddit or BitcoinTalk. Refer to financial and economic magazines and blogs for gathering all the necessary information.

Things to consider

Before you think about trading, there are a couple of things that you need to take into consideration. You should do your homework about the following things before you make your first trade.

Fees:

Most of the exchanges do provide information about the chargeable fees on a transaction, and you should be able to find this on the related website. Before joining a platform, make sure that you understand their policies regarding deposits, transactions, and even withdrawal fees. Depending on the exchange and your usage, the fees can vary substantially.

Verification:

Most of the trading platforms located in the US and UK require some form of ID proof for making deposits and withdrawals. There are some that provide anonymity. The process of verification can take up to a couple of days, and it might seem a little troublesome. But it is in your interest, and it helps in protecting the exchange from the possibility of theft, fraud, and other scams.

Mode of payment:

Understand the different modes of payment that are provided by the exchange. Maybe they use credit cards, debit cards, wire transfers, or even PayPal. If an exchange has restricted or limited payment options, then it might not be the most convenient option available for you. Whenever you want to purchase any cryptocurrency with your credit card, then you will need to verify your identity, and this also comes with a higher transaction and processing fees. Also, the risk of fraud is higher too. Acquiring cryptocurrency through a wire transfer can take a while since it needs to be processed and verified by the concerned bank first.

Exchange rate:

Different exchanges have different exchange rates. You will probably be surprised about the amount that you can save by doing a little bit of research. At times, the exchange rates can go up to 10% or even higher. So, do your research carefully.

Geographical restrictions:

There are a few user-specific functions like an exchange offer, which is accessible only in certain countries. Make sure that the exchange you are opting for provides complete access to all tools and functions regardless of the country you are located in.

Finding a Market

A Trading Platform is built to allow for a stock market exchange of currencies, and this is what you normally want when you are buying and selling currencies as a hobby or profession. Personal trading leads to scams, bad deals, and is viewed as only something you do if you need a quick way in the game or you need to buy a product/service. There are a few things to be aware of:

- There's going to be a lot of identification requirements unless you go with an anonymous exchange, but then you risk losing money if the exchange gets into any trouble or is, itself, a scam. Identification gives you protection from your government a good portion of the time.

- If you plan to use credit cards, be prepared for some very high fees. The fraudulent want to get into this game too, and so you will find many people using stolen credit cards in an attempt to get into the market. If a website doesn't provide much verification, I would be leery of investing in the platform.

- Pay attention to the exchange rate because many markets could easily take a huge portion of your value.

- Some countries have created their form of cryptocurrencies, and some others have banned the use of them, so be prepared to look at some legalese for countries you want to trade in.

Best cryptocurrency exchanges in the Market

ShapeShift

Cryptocurrencies only. You have to have them to use this platform, but it has the best support when it comes to trading for them. However, it is also possible to trade without an account on this market as well so beware your choices on the platform. It's considered a good platform, but that doesn't mean everyone comes out happy.

Bitsquare:

This is an easy-to-use and user-friendly peer-to-peer exchange that allows the users to buy and sell their Bitcoins in exchange for other cryptocurrencies or even fiat currencies. It markets itself a decentralized peer-to-peer platform and is accessible instantly and doesn't need any registration and indeed doesn't depend on a central authority. This platform never holds onto the funds of the user expect the trading partners who an exchange their data. The platform provides good security coupled with MultiSigna addresses, a security deposit, and a self-built arbitration system for solving any trading disputes. If anonymity is a high priority for you, then this is a wonderful platform for you.

Kraken

This is another popular one, again, but, also again, it's very limited. The platform is a bit clunky and is difficult to get used to, but at least this one allows you to have a chance in trading in many of the other Altcoins.

Coinbase

It's limited, but it's the one with the most reputation. It deals with only three currencies right now, which could be a problem if you plan to go after Altcoins, but it does support Ether and Litecoin.

Poloniex:

It is one of the most popular cryptocurrency exchanges, and it was founded in the year 2014. The transaction provides a secured trading platform with over 100 Bitcoin-cryptocurrency pairings and several advanced tools and data analysis as well. This trading platform has one of the highest trading volumes recorded, and the users always have the option of closing their trade position.

Bitstamp:

This is a European Union Bitcoin marketplace that was created in 2011. This platform is amongst the first-gen Bitcoin exchanges that have managed to develop a loyal customer base for itself. It is a well-known and quite trusted throughout the Bitcoin community and is a very safe platform. It offers several security features like the two-step authentication procedure and the multi-signature technology for its cryptocurrency wallet and has a cold storage that is fully insured. It offers 24/7 customer support to its users, and the user interface is multilingual.

LocalBitcoin:

This is a peer-to-peer Bitcoin exchange, and the buyers and sellers are located all over the world. By using this platform, you have the option of meeting up with others in your surroundings for trading in Bitcoins for cash, sending money through PayPal, Skrill, or Dwolla, or even arrange for the required amount to be deposited at a bank branch.

CoinMama:

This is a veteran broker exchange, and anyone can visit it for buying Bitcoin or Ethereum by making use of credit cards or cash via MoneyGram or the Western Union. This was created for those who would like to make an instant or a straightforward purchase of digital currency by using the local fiat currency. This service is available to users all over the world, but there are some countries where the users might not be able to access all the functions provided by this website. The user interface is available in several languages like English, German, French, Russian, and Italian as well.

CHAPTER 11

HOW TO INVEST IN CRYPTOCURRENCY

When it comes to investing in cryptocurrencies, there are three basic activities, and these are buying, selling and holding cryptocurrencies. Everything connected to cryptocurrency investment is based on these three activities. At the heart of the matter is the simple principle of "buying low" and "selling high." What this simply means is buying coins at a low price and selling at a higher price to make a profit. That is just it, as simple as that but is it that simple in reality? Well, the truth is an investment in cryptocurrencies can seem daunting to the uninitiated at first, what with the sheer volume of information that must be understood and the high price volatility that seems to be a constant feature of the market. Add to this, the many instances of fraud surrounding some coins on the market and a few people get rightly frightened at getting anywhere near the market.

However, people have made fortunes investing in the cryptocurrency market and not just early adopters only. What is required is the willingness to understand the unique nature of the market and following tried and tested guidelines to help you navigate the cryptocurrency market so that you can make good profits. Just like other forms of investments like stocks and bonds, cryptocurrencies require specific tools for success, without which you cannot hope to take advantage of the market adequately. Before going into the intricacies of trading in cryptocurrencies, there is one crucial aspect of being in the cryptocurrency world that must be attended to. This crucial aspect is, of course, the thing that is known as cryptocurrency wallets.

If you are new to the cryptocurrency investment scene, it is perhaps wiser to use Coinbase (if you are American) or any other reputable wallet-exchange hybrid company to keep things simple. When you begin to get the hang of the process, you can diversify your portfolio to include other exchanges that offer other crypto coins. Even if you are an expert trader in stocks and bonds, cryptocurrencies are a different matter entirely, so it is best to start small.

Using Coinbase as an example, the following are the steps that will be taken when trading cryptocurrencies.

Step One

You will have to sign up with Coinbase by visiting their website. You open an account with Coinbase, and your journey begins. You have the option of using their wallet service or choosing to use your hardware wallet. Using your hardware wallet is highly recommended.

Step Two

The second step involves selecting your payment method. Coinbase offers numerous payment methods such as bank account, debit card, and credit card. This makes exchanging crypto coin for your local currency and vice-versa a lot easier. Be sure to take a look at the fees for each payment option before deciding on the one to use. Also, pay attention to the approval time interval, i.e., how long it will take for your payments to be approved.

Step Three

Once your payment method is approved, you can begin to buy cryptocurrencies. On Coinbase you can buy Bitcoin, Ethereum, and Litecoin. Once you buy your first crypto coins, the trading process commences where you make decisions on when to sell, exchange, or hold. As you progressively get better at trading, you will want to sign up with another exchange platform and begin to perform exchanges between different cryptocurrencies.

A few things to keep in mind

1. Government Regulation.

In many countries, there isn't a well-defined legal policy on cryptocurrencies. Some countries are friendly towards it while others are downright hostile with a few not coming out to promote or a clampdown on cryptocurrencies. It is a good idea to get an understanding of the position of the government in your country when it comes to cryptocurrencies so as not to run afoul of the law and lose your investments in the process.

2. Adequate Research.

Bitcoin, Ethereum, and Litecoin have experienced some form of growth and stability in the past few months. New crypto coin offerings are notorious for sprouting almost every day boasting unrealistic benefits. Before investing in any of these new cryptocurrencies, be sure to do adequate research. Don't be hesitant to rely on expert opinions but be sure that you are following unbiased experts like can be found on Coincap and Blockfolio.

3. Volatility.

Cryptocurrencies are highly volatile. The market experiences incredible fluctuations in prices and as such great care must be taken when making decisions based on current market value.

CHAPTER 12

BENEFITS AND RISKS OF INVESTING

Benefits

Lower Cost of Transactions

While frozen accounts may be problematic, you also need to be aware of the cost of getting a transaction ready for use. On top of the unexpected risks of frozen accounts and massive chargebacks when you use payment processors, you will also be exposed to well-known high transaction charges for the services of these payment processors. This can considerably reduce the income of your business.

The transaction charges of PayPal, Google Checkout, and Amazon Checkout all begin at 2.9 percent plus $ 0.30 for each transaction. You can enjoy a lower rate of 1.9 percent only if your total transactions for the monthly amount to more than $ 30,000. Because of this, these exorbitant fees may burden business with a low-profit-margin. The same goes for businesses that require a lot of smaller transactions or those whose products are sold at a nominal price.

Financial Self-Determinism and Control

The cryptocurrency networks are one of a kind because they are a digital store of value where people can securely save cryptocurrency units and enter into transactions without the need to rely on any third party regulatory body. After you have acquired and safely secured your cryptocurrency units, it is almost impossible for other people (thieves, hackers, banks or even the government) to take them away from you. The government cannot authorize the freezing of your cryptocurrency account nor stop you from entering into any transactions within the cryptocurrency network. This is the primary reason why people love cryptocurrencies because the lack of regulation allows free movement of money. The government can only do as much as track cryptocurrency purchases with fiat currencies, but they cannot track purchases using cryptocurrencies by the individual.

It Works Around the World

The cryptocurrency network is considered to be an intrinsically wide-reaching and global network. One of the biggest arguments for cryptocurrencies is the fast and low-cost transaction speeds across the world. You will not have to pass through artificial barriers to make payments to vendors who are based in other countries or regions. In fact, it is not entirely possible to validate where a particular cryptocurrency transaction originated. An online vendor who accepts cryptocurrency units as a mode of payment can instantly gain access to a global market while facing the risk of non-payment from customers who reside outside his own country and who are not bound by the legal system of his government.

Risks

Know what you're investing in.

One thing is for certain that the relatively anonymous nature of cryptocurrencies is a huge part of what allows people to adjust the values of cryptocurrencies as they see fit. This makes for an added risk to the cryptocurrency. Of course, whoever is regulating it could always stop doing so and focus on some other kind of investment in the future, but it can be near impossible to figure out what's going to happen.

Volatility of Cryptocurrency Prices

When does someone ask you what the value of the cryptocurrency units that you own is, how can you readily answer the question? The fundamental value of any particular currency is a function of the consumer demand for that currency and the consumers' capability to use the currency to trade it for valuable goods and services. Because a lot of conventional currencies are no longer linked to the worth of an underlying product or commodity such as gold and other precious metals, a cryptocurrency unit will only be valuable when some people or consumers want to own them and use them for trade. So if one day the world decides there is no longer a need for cryptocurrencies, the prices will plummet. Though this is unlikely, it is still a potential risk.

Regulatory Ambiguity

The legal category of cryptocurrencies remains uncertain. Some people consider it as a commodity like gold and silver while others treat it as a viable currency. Still, there are others who look at them as a financial product or something that is legally equal to the gold in World of Warcraft. It is yet to be known if they will someday require licenses and financial rules and regulations for it to become a truly viable currency.

Risk of Loss

When you own cryptocurrency units, it is quite apparent that you have the responsibility to ensure that your digital wallet is secured from any potential hazards of loss and theft. This task or responsibility can be quite taxing, especially if you own a substantial number of cryptocurrencies because you will have to use certain tools such as protected encryption, password management, and information backup to make sure that your risks are maintained at a low-level.

Several high-profile incidents have already been reported where people made errors and mistakes in handling their cryptocurrency accounts that ultimately led to them losing a large number of their cryptocurrencies. Since there is no central authority you can approach to seek help or assistance, you may have to completely write off your losses because they may already be unrecoverable.

The risks associated with cryptocurrencies are critical and have to be identified. It should not be a surprise that a virtual currency that is relatively new is in danger of being hacked into. You should be cautious when seeing how this currency is run before you make any trades with it.

Things to consider.

- Consider a hardware device. Keeping your funds offline can be added protection. However, the risk of losing your hard-wallet is likely.

- Although it may seem common sense, NEVER hand out your private keys to anyone. The private keys given by any wallet is the code that allows direct access to your cryptocurrencies.

- Never leave funds on exchanges. If you've been in the cryptocurrency world for a while, you would know several major hacks in the past that have resulted in multi-million dollar loses. Most notably the Mt. Gox hack.

Additionally, leaving your cryptocurrencies on exchanges leaves your funds subject to the exchanges' rules. A good example is an incident on 1st August 2017, with the introduction of Bitcoin Cash. Any Bitcoin owned on Coinbase is subject to Coinbase' terms and conditions. Coinbase chose not to give any Bitcoin Cash to any Bitcoin owners during the Bitcoin hard for. Exchanges are not liable for any loss that has occurred, so protect yourself.

CHAPTER 13

CRYPTOCURRENCY BROKER

If you want to trade cryptocurrencies, you have to open an account with a reliable cryptocurrency trading broker. Now, by simply searching online, you will find lots of brokers that seem to offer the same services. So, how do you know which broker you should use and will best suit your needs? Here is a set of standards to look for:

A note about using a trading broker

You are not always required to use a trading broker. If you intend to trade cryptocurrencies, then you need a trading broker. However, if you just want to invest, say, in bitcoin, especially if it is a long-term investment, then all you need is to get a cryptocurrency wallet. There are cryptocurrency wallets like Coinbase and coins.ph that allow their users to buy bitcoins directly from the wallet itself. Hence, if you just want to make a long-term investment in bitcoin, then you might just get a bitcoin wallet and skip the party where you need to use a trading broker.

Mobile version

These days, it is easier and quicker to access the Internet using your mobile phone. Hence, your broker should allow you to access the trading platform directly from your mobile device. You should be able to manage your account and open and close positions using your mobile phone. Your broker should also make it easy and convenient for you to do this. The important parts of the trading platform should be easily accessible on your mobile device. The mobile version should be as convenient, if not more convenient, as the desktop version.

Deposit and withdrawal limits and requirements

Find out the minimum and maximum limit for making a deposit and withdrawal. Also, it is common for brokers to ask for a copy of certain documents before they process a withdrawal. Be sure that you have these documents available in your possession; otherwise, you run the risk of having your cryptocurrencies locked in your trading account without any way of withdrawing them or turning them into real money. Make sure that you know the requirements of your broker. It is fairly easy to make a deposit, but it can be hard to make a withdrawal.

Fees

Check the fees that your broker may impose. Is there a trading fee? Is there a fixed amount that is imposed or is there a certain percentage? Also, check how much is the withdrawal fee. Pay attention to other fees that your broker might impose.

Customer support

It is important for you to work with a broker that has an active and professional customer support team. Find out the ways that your broker offers on how to keep in touch with the support team. Normally, there is an email address that you can contact, or you can even send a message directly to the broker's trading platform. Your brawler may also provide you with a number that you can call or even an on-page love chat support. Also, check the schedule as to the availability of the customer support.

Trading platform

Your broker should provide you with a professionally designed trading platform. Although design itself is not that important, it also helps to set the mood for trading. The trading platform should also provide you with tools that you need, such as graphs and charts, to help you come up with a sound trading decision. The platform should also be easy and convenient to use. All in all, it should make the trading experience easier and more comfortable for you.

Latest ratings and reviews

Before you despair any real money or cryptocurrency in your trading account, you should first check the latest ratings and reviews of your chosen broker as given by other traders. Doing this is easy. Simply use your favorite browser, type the name of the broker, and add the word "reviews." Press the enter key and wait for the search engine results page (SERP) to give you a list of related pages. Read as many reviews as you cab from different websites and reviewers.

Cryptocurrencies being traded

Check the cryptocurrencies that are available for trading. Of course, the more cryptocurrencies that your broker provides, the more choices that you will have. Ideally, your broker should also make available the not so known altcoins. After all, many of these unpopular altcoins also increase in price significantly. Hence, if you are a trader, you should also keep your eyes on them. Some of these altcoins have even increased by more than 1,000%.

Bonuses

Check if the broker offers useful bonuses and promos. Bonuses or promos are not required, but they can be helpful. Just be careful before you accept any bonus or promo since it usually comes with a catch. For example, there is usually a requirement that you need to meet before you can make a withdrawal. Unfortunately, such requirement is not always easy to satisfy. Therefore, before you accept and bonus or promo, be sure that the terms and conditions of the bonus are clear to you. In case of doubt, feel free to contact the customer support team.

Margin trading

A trading broker may also allow you to do margin trading. Margin trading is where you can borrow cryptocurrencies from the broker so that you can trade and hopefully profit a higher amount. Of course, since you will be borrowing cryptocurrencies from your broker, you will have to pay your broker a certain interest. Normally, a broker may allow you to margin trade more than 50% of your invested capital. Find out how much you can margin trade and the interest imposed by your broker. Take note that if you are a beginner, it is advised that you should avoid margin trading.

CHAPTER 14

STRATEGIES FOR RISK MINIMIZATION

Investing is risky in general and investing in cryptocurrencies is a high-risk, high return activity. At present, there is no other category of investment that has potential as high as the one offered by cryptocurrencies. However, with high rewards, the risk involved is quite high too. As a crypto investor, there are a couple of risks that you should be aware of.

Liquidity risk

Another challenge that investors who are investing in mid-cap and small-cap coins are the risk of liquidity. At present, the average trading volume of Bitcoin per day is over $2 billion. If you leave the ten largest cryptos according to their market share, investors are left with a trading volume that's less than $100 million daily, and in most of the cases, it is less than $10 million. Anyone who is looking to make a more significant investment will find this situation quite challenging. Not just that, the trading volumes of the cryptos are spread over different exchanges, and it makes it quite tricky to execute a large order. To mitigate the risk posed by liquidity, try sticking to those cryptos that are quite liquid, especially when you are trading in large volumes.

Market risks

Cryptocurrencies and all kinds of digital tokens are considered to be extremely volatile. The volatility of Bitcoins has relatively reduced over the years, but all the other forms of cryptocurrencies experience intra-day price movements that can move in either direction. The market for cryptocurrencies is news-driven, and every crypto has its risk, rumors, sensationalized headlines and spiteful media campaigns by the rival blockchain technologies which can result in significant price drops and unfavorable fluctuations in the value of the cryptocurrencies. As an investor, you can significantly reduce your market risk by diversifying your investment portfolio. Your portfolio of cryptocurrencies shouldn't consist of just one form of crypto and should have smallholdings of other altcoins as well. You can further reduce your market risk by hedging your investment portfolio with BTC futures as well.

Cybersecurity risk

Regardless of what you would like to believe, if you are investing in cryptocurrencies, you are a target for hackers. Most of the digitized currencies are pseudonymous, and this makes them an ideal target for cybercriminals out there. Unfortunately, the crypto space is filled with fake websites, fraudulent email campaigns, and targeted hacking of vulnerable trading platforms. A significant risk that crypto investors should be aware of is cybercrime. There are no generalized tips for mitigating this risk and, as an investor, you should take all the necessary steps to ensure the cyber-safety of your investments and holdings.

Fraud risk

Numerous schemes promise unrealistically high returns and are often promoted across different social media platforms and at times are even advertised on reputable cryptocurrency media outlets. Usually, these are just pyramid schemes. However, scammers keep coming up with fraudulent ICOs to scam novice investors. Prudence and research can prevent you from falling prey to such scams. Make sure that you are doing your research and aren't investing because someone asked or told you to.

Well, it might seem like there are plenty of risks that you might have to face as an investor, but you can successfully mitigate your chances by taking a couple of simple steps. Make sure that you keep these risks in mind before entering the cryptocurrency.

Regulatory risk

Cryptocurrencies are a decentralized form of currencies. However, regulatory uncertainty poses a significant hurdle for any seller. Whenever a considerable cryptocurrency trading platform announces any adverse cryptocurrency norms, the entire market gets shaken. For instance, China has recently proclaimed a ban on

ICOs (initial coin offerings), and this caused a significant drop in the prices of Chinese digital currencies like NEO. Regulatory risk isn't just confined to one region of the world. All those who are investing in cryptocurrencies should follow any legal news about the tokens they are investing in quite regularly. At present, the major governments of the world haven't banned the use of cryptocurrencies. However, if they do so, then the effect can be devastating. Sadly, regulatory risk cannot be mitigated, and all that an investor can do is follow the news closely and act by what they learn.

Operational risk

When it comes to trading cryptocurrencies and storing funds, operational risks are bound to exist. The major centralized Bitcoin exchanges happen to be frequent targets for cybercriminals. Even if you are making use of own wallets to store your funds, you might still suffer a loss if you don't store your holdings in cold storage. If you are interested in minimizing the operational risk you face, then you should make use of decentralized exchanges and opt for hardware wallets while storing your funds.

CHAPTER 15

POWERFUL STRATEGIES

Technical Analysis

Technical analysis is used by many cryptocurrency investors and traders. If you are more of a visual person and enjoy analyzing graphs and charts, then the technical analysis is the one for you. With technical analysis, you will be dealing with the price movements as reflected by the graphs and charts. The idea behind this approach is that all the different factors that affect a cryptocurrency have their final influence on the price. Therefore, by simply dealing with the price movement alone, you get to analyze the many factors that affect a cryptocurrency all at once. Also, regardless of how many factors that you analyze, it is still the price movement of a cryptocurrency that will determine whether or not you will make a profit.

The key to using technical analysis is to be able to identify patterns. Indeed, patterns do exist. However, you should remember that patterns come and go. Therefore, do not expect to see a pattern every time that you look at a chart or graph. But, if ever you see one, then you should take advantage of it.

Quick Sell

This strategy relies on small yet continuous profits. When you use this strategy, it is important for you to exercise discipline and not be greedy. So, how does it work? The key is to close your position as soon as you experience a small profit. This way you can effectively minimize your risk and exposure.

When you use this strategy, it is also advised that you use a stop-loss limit, so that you will know just up to what price you will continue to keep your investment. If you reach this limit, then accept losses and do not hesitate to close your position. This strategy is not hard to do, but you have to apply proper timing and be sure to close your position way before the price behavior changes. Again, you should not be greedy. Stick to earning continuous and small profits.

Fundamental Analysis

When it comes to any form of investing, fundamental analysis us something that you should learn. Many people consider it as the lifeblood of investment. Where he investing in cryptocurrency, stocks, or bonds, this type of analysis always plays a vital role to your success. Fundamental analysis can also be combined with other strategies. In fact, if you consider yourself a professional cryptocurrency investor or trader, it is a must that you always apply fundamental analysis regardless of your preferred strategy for investing. After all, fundamental analysis would not harm you but can significantly help you come up with a sound investment/trading decision. Applying fundamental analysis is also what makes your investment different from gambling. Indeed, with the proper use of this strategy, you can effectively turn the odds in your favor.

Averaging Down

This strategy is a good way to earn a big amount of profit. Take note, however, that this is considered an aggressive approach, so use it carefully and wisely. Averaging down will allow you to purchase a cryptocurrency at a "bargain" which you can then sell for a profit after some time. It is not a "bargain" in the literal sense of the word.

Before you use this strategy, it is important for you to identify a cryptocurrency whose value will most likely increase in the long run. For this purpose, you may want to use fundamental analysis.

Coin Mastery

It is true that the more that you know and understand a particular cryptocurrency, the more likely that you can predict its price movement. This is exactly the focus of this strategy. When you use this approach, the key is to specialize in a single cryptocurrency of your choice. Make it a priority to find out as much as you can about that cryptocurrency. Be sure to research on it on a daily basis. Also, be updated with the latest news and developments regarding your chosen cryptocurrency. The important thing here is to achieve mastery over the cryptocurrency. This may take weeks and even months, but it is well worth it. After some time, you will notice that you are more able to predict its price movement. Once you achieve this level of understanding, then you can now make appropriate investments to make a profit. If you are convinced that you already have mastery over a particular cryptocurrency, them feel free to master another cryptocurrency. It should also be noted that while studying a particular cryptocurrency, you may realize that it is not a good investment at all. If you are sure about this, then feel free to abandon it and switch to another cryptocurrency that appears to be profitable.

Go with the Flow

When China declared that it would close down all its local cryptocurrency exchanges, the price of bitcoin fell significantly. When Singapore issued that it will not yet impose any restriction on the use of cryptocurrencies, the price of bitcoin and other altcoins increased. When CNN featured a positive news piece that shows that bitcoin is a good investment, the price of bitcoin surged higher. When Russia decided to welcome the use of bitcoin finally, its price increased. As you can see, it is not difficult to predict how the price of a cryptocurrency will move. When there is positive news about a certain cryptocurrency, it tends to draw attention and interest. Usually, this will make the price of the cryptocurrency concerned to go higher. But, in case of bad news, then the contrary can be expected. When the co-founder of bitcoin sold his coins and invested in bitcoin cash, many people followed him. As a result, the price of bitcoin dropped, and the price of bitcoin cash increased significantly. The key to using this strategy is to get as much information as you can and see how such information will lead the market. Take note that it is not always advisable to just go with the flow all the time. You also need to analyze what is going on in the market.

Altcoin Spread Out

It is not a secret that you can make a big amount of profit by investing in altcoins. Some altcoins can increase by more than 500% in price within just a few weeks. In fact, many of such altcoins are almost unheard of. They operate without drawing so much attention but are highly lucrative investments. This strategy takes advantage of this kind of altcoins. The key is to spread your investments among different altcoins that have a high-profit potential. You do not have to profit from all of these investments. For example, if you make three different investments but make a 400% profit with one of them, even if you lose your other two investments, you will still end up at a profit. It is noteworthy that some altcoins even increase by more than 1,000%.

Buy and Hold

The buy and hold strategy is a very simple strategy but is also highly effective. In fact, many of the people who became multi-millionaires by investing in cryptocurrency used this strategy. So, how does it work? As the name implies, the buy and hold strategy means buying a particular cryptocurrency and then holding on to it as you wait for its price to increase. You can then sell it for profit after some time. Just how profitable can this strategy be? Again, let us use a classic example: Had you invested even just $400 in bitcoin way back in 2010, then you would have been a multimillionaire by now. Yes, this is how effective this strategy is.

CONCLUSION

Cryptocurrency has been skyrocketing in popularity. Many people and businesses are now using this modern digital currency for different transactions. While there are some that are still skeptical about cryptocurrencies, there are a lot of people seeing potentials for digital currencies to take over traditional currencies.

If you are going to invest in cryptocurrencies, the first thing to focus on is research. You have to make judgments for yourself instead of relying on all the information that you have been given. It is after all your money – make sure that you're investing in something worthwhile. So, always look into the history, future and trade practices of the cryptocurrency before making any decisions.

You should also remember that you don't need to invest in only the famous cryptocurrencies. Everybody knows about Bitcoin, and they all want to get in on it. This means that the returns on Bitcoin might not be as good because even Bitcoin at this point requires a hefty sum of initial investment.

You should focus on the upcoming small players like OmiseGO, Ripple, and Golem. These platforms are highly undervalued considering the potential they have. You can invest in them now at a low price to enjoy the benefits when they blow up.

Cryptocurrencies are a helpful and innovative way of digital fund transfer. However, many negative elements in the society use it for making illicit payments. Always forbid from using your Cryptocurrency for anything that is prohibited by laws in your country or international laws.

Always keep your passwords and keys securely with you. Do not share the private keys with anyone. The implications of this could be quite hazardous. All your money could be stolen, or even worse, used illegally.

With that said, using Cryptocurrency is like adjusting to the speed of the modern and the futuristic world. Cryptocurrencies are the way to transfer money in today's world. Not only it is secure, but the benefits are paramount.

Cryptocurrencies are a wonderful invention and, within a short span of time, they have managed to revolutionize the entire financial system of different economies. By now you will have realized that investing in cryptocurrencies is beneficial and all the benefits they provide the holder with. Make use of the information provided in this book for making your trade without having to rely on any guesswork. It takes a while to get the hang of this new technology, but the returns will undoubtedly make it worth your while. Move overstocks and real estate, the future of investing lies in cryptocurrencies.

This is your chance to be part of the fastest growing innovation this world has ever seen, and if you do, you will be glad you did. If you would like to invest in cryptocurrency after reading this book . Checkout coinbase.com and download the coinbase app .

THE END !!!

Congratulations !!!

You have just finished the book . I hope you are fully aware of how cryptocurrencies work . The goal I had in mind was to teach you the basics of cryptocurrencies, and I hope that's what this book did for you . If you want to further educate yourself on the topic . By all means go for it, but hopefully you understand that this book does not have the expert level tips or strategies to make you a millionaire tomorrow . I definitely hope you liked this book and you learned something.

Can i ask you for a favor? Will you please be kind enough to leave an honest review at the end of this book . THANK YOU !!!

If you would like to contact me to discuss something or would like to offer me some advice this is my email :

cbashsuperdome@gmail.com

Please Checkout my other books on Amazon :

Billionaire Habits : How Ultra Wealthy People Move

https://www.amazon.com/Billionaires-Habits-Ultra-Wealthy-People-ebook/dp/B07B5WJHZY

Financial Planning and Debt Management: How to Plan a Successful Life

https://www.amazon.comPFinancial-Planning-Debt-Plan-Successful-ebook/dp/B077LF3YV2

The Awesome Power of Social Media: How Social Media has Changed Everything

https://www.amazon.com/Financial-Planning-Debt-Plan-Successful-ebook/dp/B077LF3YV2

The Power of Perseverance: Proven Steps and Strategies of Achieving Success Through Perseverance

https://www.amazon.com/Power-Perseverance-Strategies-Achieving-Success-ebook/dp/B078WLFBZN

www.ingramcontent.com/pod-product-compliance
Lightning Source LLC
Chambersburg PA
CBHW070212230526
45471CB00002B/930